Mr. & Mrs. Richard Rodgers   Louis Lotito   Dave Garroway   Henry Hewes, Saturday Review   Mr. & Mrs. Lawrence Langner
Mr. & Mrs. Oscar Hammerstein   Mainbocher   Robert Coleman, N. Y. Daily Mirror   Frank Aston, N. Y. World-Telegram Sun   (Armina Marshall)
exander Ince, Theatre Arts   Dorothy Gish   Danton Walker, N. Y. Daily News
. & Mrs. Al Hirschfeld,   Lillian Gish   Valentina   Hope Hampton   Theresa Helburn   Mr. & Mrs. Billy Rose
N. Y. Times (Dolly Haas)   Mr. & Mrs. Ira Katzenberg   (Joyce Mathews)

THE AMERICAN THEATRE

THE AMERICAN THEATRE

AS SEEN BY

GEORGE BRAZILLER   NEW YORK   1961

I wish to acknowledge my indebtedness to the proprietors of *The New York Times* for kindly allowing me to reproduce the bulk of the drawings in this book which originally appeared in their paper. A bow of gratitude is also extended to the New York *Herald Tribune* and *Theatre Arts* for permission to reproduce drawings from their publications, to Carol Channing for the front curtain of SHOW GIRL, to Alexander Cohen for the front curtain of AT THE DROP OF A HAT, and to William Zeckendorf for the mural of "First Nighters" in the Playbill Room of the Hotel Manhattan, New York City.

Library of Congress Catalog Card Number 61-15495

FIRST PRINTING

Lithographed in the United States of America by The Murray Printing Co., Forge Village, Mass.

For FRED ALLEN, old and dear friend who summed up the achievements of a full creative life—
"I am probably the only writer in the world who has written more than he can lift."

BROOKS ATKINSON, longhand writer, at work

AL, THE BEARD

By BROOKS ATKINSON

For the last twelve years these coolly organized drawings have emanated from a littered studio on the top floor of a brownstone-front house in East Ninety-Fifth Street. There is a tiny skylight in the rear, big enough for a roofing mechanic to struggle through. But the main light comes from a wide bank of windows that survey the chimneys and television aerials across the street.

The floor is piled with drawings, some of them in heaps, some laid out individually as if for study. Every flat surface in the studio is deep in photographs or magazines. A loose-jointed rack, leaning to starboard, contains piles of periodicals and some books, including Rabelais. A puppet, two masks and a jumble of posters hang on the walls.

The grimy drawing board looks like a butcher's block, so many sheets of bristol board have been hacked on it with a knife. A mouldy barber-chair, with a well-scuffed footrest, pokes the artist close to the drawing board.

Until about 5:30 in the afternoon, when Al Hirschfeld is summoned by buzzer to come downstairs for refreshments, he is likely to be at work in this hurrahs-nest, making a permanent impression on the world of art. Thousands of people are entertained by his drawings in books, magazines and newspapers — especially readers of the Sunday drama section of *The New York Times*. Al has been giving it a racy appearance for more than thirty years.

But some people who study them carefully realize that, in addition to being amusing, they are works of art, and many of them masterpieces. In the field of calligraphy, Al is a genius. He is a master of line, perspective and design. The principal museums in America buy his drawings because they are not only vivid records of people everyone knows but also part of the twentieth century. Manners and styles will change. But Al's drawings will remain, like those of Cruikshank, Daumier and Toulouse-Lautrec, as records of a way of life by an artist who has a point of view.

Although the point of view is critical it is also full of enjoyment. For Al is very much a man of his time; he enjoys the insanities of the moment. He lives in the midst of them with enthusiasm. About many aspects of modern life, he is a cynic; he loves to startle people with paradoxical declarations on a sweeping scale. But with his wife, Dolly Haas, and their daughter, Nina, he lives a gregarious life that he thoroughly enjoys, especially when it is crack-brained. The vigor and confidence of his lines reveal the strength of his character.

Whether the drawings are to be called caricatures or character sketches is an arguable point. Since his portraits of people are comic, they are generally described as caricatures. But they would not have enduring value as art if they were merely clever distortions of nature. Al has no patience with anatomical caricature. If a man's most conspicuous feature is a big nose, Al will make a point of ignoring it or placing the emphasis elsewhere. Deficiencies in a person's appearance do not interest him.

What he is looking for is something that expresses the total personality. He says that you can recognize a person you know when you see him so far away that his features cannot be identified. You can pick him out of a crowd even when you cannot see him clearly. Sometimes you can recognize him when his back is all that you see. For his total personality is greater than the sum of his features.

That is what Al tries to capture. His comic exaggerations are not so much distortions of fact as enlargements of the total personality. Although his drawings are fantastifications, they are from the inside out. Instead of burlesquing people, he joins them on their own terms, adding his own gaiety for good measure. He is a portrait artist. He is more interested in the nature of his subjects than in making fun of them. There is an element of clairvoyance in his work. You recognize his people, though you would swear that he is being outrageous. One of Al's drawings is so penetrating that Ray Bolger says he has been trying to imitate it ever since it appeared. It shows him what he wants to do.

When Al is making a drawing for the drama section of the Sunday edition of the *Times*, he normally sees a performance out of town, in Washington, Philadelphia, New Haven, Boston or some more distant city. Sitting in the audience in a dark theatre, he makes a series of sketches of the actors —profile, full-face or both. While he is sketching he is also trying to invent in his mind an over-all design that will give an impression of the play, on the one hand, and on the other, emerge as a considered work of art.

In his studio he draws the complete picture in pencil, struggling not to lose the freshness of the sketches. When he concludes that the picture is as good as he can do under the circumstances, he draws the final lines in ink and then erases the pencil marks. That's the technique.

But the art goes beyond skill. It consists in the understanding Al has of the people he is drawing in the center of a bizarre world. Although the drawings are seldom flattering, most of his subjects value them because they recognize in his wild swirl of lines a vivid streak of the truth. Al's sense of humor does not impair the seriousness of his artistic purpose.

THE TWENTIES

I lived and painted in Paris during most of the Twenties, occasionally returning to New York to "look around" and add to my collection of contemporary money. On one of these infrequent sojourns back to my native land to get a fresh shirt, I found myself in the theatre one evening watching a performance of the celebrated French actor, Sacha Guitry, in his debut in the American theatre. During the performance I doodled a likeness of Mr. Guitry on the back of the theatre program. My companion, seated next to me, seemed impressed with my scribble. He suggested that I translate this drawing onto a clean sheet of paper and he would personally take it to a friend of his who worked on the New York *Herald Tribune*.

Needless to say, I did the drawing on virgin drawing board and the following Sunday, larger than life, there it was on the cover of the *Herald Tribune*'s Sunday drama page. Encouraged by Arthur Folwell, George Goldsmith and Mark Goodrich, who comprised the editorial staff of the *Herald Tribune* drama department, I made a weekly contribution to the Sunday edition of that paper for the next twenty years.

One day, sometime in the mid-Twenties, I received the following telegram:

WOULD LIKE A DRAWING OF HARRY LAUDER TWO COLS 4½ INCHES DEEP DELIVERY NO LATER THAN TUESDAY   SAM ZOLOTOW NEW YORK TIMES

I phoned Mr. Zolotow to make certain the assignment was on the level and not an impractical joke invented by one of my screwball friends. Assured that the commission was a legitimate one I did the drawing (reproduced on opposite page) of Sir Harry Lauder and delivered it to an elderly man seated behind the reception desk at the *Times*. The two-column drawing appeared the following Sunday on the *Times* drama page. For the ensuing two years I was assigned via Western Union to do either a three-, four- or five-column drawing of specific personalities, which I would dutifully deposit with the old man at the *Times* reception desk. I never met or spoke to anyone connected with the paper, during those years, except this anonymous gent.

One evening, at intermission, as I was standing in a theatre lobby chatting with the show's press agent, Dick Maney, a stranger ambled over and joined our conversation. Maney said in a matter of fact way, "You fellows know each other." We stared at each other, the stranger and I, without recognition. In the embarrassed silence Dick Maney, whose eyebrows seemed to have left his forehead in surprise, introduced me to Sam Zolotow.

I tell this story of my advent into the Art of Caricature and subsequent introduction to the complex publishing field to illustrate to my reader that neither my life nor this book fits a rigid plan. The reason for the sparse collection of drawings in this chapter is that these are the only ones I could reasonably lay my hands on. Moral for younger artists . . . keep a filing cabinet handy.

Sir Harry Lauder returned to Broadway for the
first of his innumerable farewell performances.

Florence Reed as "Mother Goddam" in THE SHANGHAI GESTURE. 1926

Jules Hatfield in THE WALTZ OF THE DOGS. 1927

Joe Cook explains why he will not imitate four Hawaiians playing the ukulele at the same time in RAIN OR SHINE. 1927

Basil Rathbone, homme fatale, in THE COMMAND TO LOVE. 1928

Albert Carrol, female impersonator, in THE GRAND STREET FOLLIES OF 1928.

Jane Cowl in the perennial THE ROAD TO ROME. 1928

Weber and Fields revive their celebrated act from Burlesque for THE LAMBS GAMBOL. 1925

THE THIRTIE$

For political reasons the Federal government padlocked its own production of THE CRADLE WILL ROCK on opening night at the Eltinge Theatre in 1937. The assembled first-nighters, including myself, were entertained in front of the darkened theatre by Marc Blitzstein (the opera's composer) playing at a mini piano on an improvised open truck, while Orson Welles (WPA producer of the show) scurried around town in a frantic search for another available threatre. About nine o'clock Mr. Welles triumphantly reappeared to announce that he had managed to book the Jolson Theatre and all tickets would be honored at the speak-easy performance to take place that night. The audience trekked enthusiastically after their leader from The Eltinge on 39th Street to The Jolson on 59th Street, but unlike the lemmings, they were amply rewarded for their loyalty.

Leaving props, scenery and costumes in the shuttered Eltinge, we (the cast and audience) eventually found ourselves seated in the Jolson staring at a bare stage. Accompanied by thunderous applause Mr. Welles and Mr. Blitzstein made their unique entrance pushing a piano on stage from the wings. Blitzstein seated himself at the piano and Welles began his unrehearsed recital of the physical properties, lighting, costumes and locale of the original production which they had worked on for almost one year. He described a sumptuous spectacle paid for by the U.S. Treasury. The stage was to have been translucent with specially designed lighting by Feder; the light source from below stage would have created the illusion of endless space with the performers suspended in it.

Having established the actual physical production with words he then announced that he would play all the parts and Mr. Blitzstein would sing the arias.

At a given signal Mr. Blitzstein struck the first chord of his revolutionary score when, to his astonishment and Mr. Welles', no less than the audience's, an actor from the cast stood up from his seat somewhere in the balcony and sang his rehearsed role. Mr. Blitzstein had only to play the music, Mr. Welles only to stand there dumbfounded and delighted, as actor after actor, scattered throughout the house, arose in his place and played his respective part. It was a memorable night in the theatre.

The drawing shows Marc Blitzstein at the piano.

Marc Blitzstein

Norman Lloyd and Paula Laurence in the WPA production, SING FOR YOUR SUPPER; Helen Hayes, unforgettable, in VICTORIA REGINA; Jimmy Savo and Teddy Hart in THE BOYS FROM SYRACUSE; Katharine Cornell and Fritz Kortner in HEROD AND MARIANNE; the incorrigible genius Orson Welles in RICHARD THE III; Dean Jagger in MISSOURI LEGEND; and Maurice Evans in HAMLET. 1938

Eva Le Gallienne in MADAME CAPET; Hiram Sherman and Philip Loeb in SING
OUT THE NEWS; Raymond Massey in ABE LINCOLN IN ILLINOIS portrayed Lin-
coln so believably that to this very day I find it easier to believe Lincoln is
still alive and appearing in the theatre under the pseudonym of Raymond
Massey; and Walter Huston who sang Kurt Weill's "September Song" in
KNICKERBOCKER HOLIDAY. 1938

Mary Jane Walsh, Philip Loeb, Joey Faye, Hiram Sherman and Dorothy Fox in SING OUT THE NEWS. 1938

Mussolini and the "Four Little Angels of Peace Are We" in Harold Rome's PINS AND NEEDLES presented by the International Ladies Garment Workers Union. 1937

Ruth Gordon in THE COUNTRY WIFE. 1936

George M. Cohan in PIGEONS AND PEOPLE. 1933

Robert Mulligan, Martin Gabel, Marjorie Main, Carroll Ashburn and Bobby Jordan in Sidney Kingsley's DEAD END. 1935

Clark and McCullough in Gershwin's STRIKE UP THE BAND. 1930

Dorothy Gish in Jed Harris' production
of THE INSPECTOR GENERAL. 1930

Sam Levene, Eddie Albert, Philip Loeb
and Teddy Hart in ROOM SERVICE. 1937

Katharine Cornell in SAINT JOAN. 1936

Alfred Lunt and Lynn Fontanne in
THE TAMING OF THE SHREW. 1935

Sophie Tucker in LEAVE IT TO ME. 1938

Imogene Coca caricatured Carmen Miranda
in THE STRAW HAT REVIEW. 1939

Alfred Lunt and Richard Whorf, from their celestial peephole, eavesdropped on Lynn Fontanne darning a sock in AMPHITRYON 38. 1937

Orson Welles and Paula Lawrence in the WPA production, DR. FAUSTUS, and Norman Lloyd in the Federal Theatre production, POWER. 1937. The original theatre technique used in staging POWER became celebrated as The Living Newspaper. This form has never again been tried either "on" or "off Broadway."

Mitzi Mayfair in THE SHOW IS ON. 1937

The Nicholas Brothers billed as "The Whizz Hoofers" in BABES IN ARMS. 1937

Paul Haakon and Evelyn Thawl in THE SHOW IS ON. 1937

Hugh Sinclair and Elizabeth Bergner (her first American appearance) in ESCAPE ME NEVER. 1935

Vilma and Buddy Ebsen, Fanny Brice, Everett Marshall and Willie Howard in THE ZIEGFELD FOLLIES. 1935

Maurice Ellis, Bill "Bojangles" Robinson and Eddie Green in Mike Todd's first Broadway production, THE HOT MIKADO. 1939

Benny Goodman, Louis "Satchmo" Armstrong, Maxine Sullivan and Butterfly McQueen in SWINGIN' THE DREAM. 1939

Guy Robertson, Blanche Ring (I've Got Rings On My Fingers and Bells On My Toes), Thelma White and Joe E. Lewis in RIGHT THIS WAY. 1938

Francine Larrimore in SHOOTING STAR. 1933

Margaret Anglin barges onstage in FRESH FIELDS. 1936

Louis Lytton as pot-bellied Sir John Falstaff in THE MERRY WIVES OF WINDSOR. 1938

Jimmy Durante played a mad Russian in STARS IN YOUR EYES. 1939

The Group Theatre did AWAKE AND SING and ROCKET TO THE MOON in their repertory theatre. These players performed in both productions. Art Smith, the father in AWAKE, consoles himself as the dentist in ROCKET. Morris Carnovsky, the husband in ROCKET tries to prevent his own suicide as the grandfather in AWAKE.

Sanford Meisner, the Hollywood gent in ROCKET, offers worldly advice to himself as the luckless husband in AWAKE. Luther Adler, young philanderer in AWAKE, studies his own reflection as an old rake in ROCKET. The fellow at the right with his arms around himself is the author of both plays, Clifford Odets. 1939

Hugh O'Connell, Jean Dixon, George S. Kaufman and Charles Halton in ONCE IN A LIFETIME. 1930

Philip Loeb, Hester Sondergaard, Sidney Lumet (destined to become one of our most gifted directors) and Art Smith in William Saroyan's first play MY HEART'S IN THE HIGHLANDS. 1939. The ensuing years were peppered with Saroyan's poetic plays . . . and then came the war. Saroyan survived the war but not the Theatre. The Theatre has never been the same since. Come back, Bill!

Should you find a way to ravel the above enigma you will discover Teddy Hart on the left and Jimmy Savo on the right in mistaken identities in THE BOYS FROM SYRACUSE. 1938

THE FORTIES

In the Forties I married Dolly Haas, World War II began and our daughter (Nina) was born 36 days after the war ended. These three seemingly unrelated facts had a profound influence on the theatre of the Forties . . . or rather, on my personal theatre of that decade. First, Dolly Haas, during most of those years, transferred her genius for the stage into baking home-made bread and broadcasting nightly as America's "Axis Dolly" over the facilities of the OWI to her former colleagues in Germany. Secondly, all of civilized humanity joined together in the greatest of all collaborations to write a third-act finale for the most stupendous spectacle ever devised by man. The War became the living theatre. And lastly, I celebrated our daughter's birth by incorporating her name in a drawing (reproduced on the page opposite) bearing the legend "Nina the Wonder Child."

Nina's name, openly but sneakily contrived to be part of the drawing, appeared for the first time. Ever since then for the past sixteen years I have included her name slyly in all of my drawings. This bit of tomfoolery became one of the worst-kept secrets in the publishing business. The game became a sort of ritual to many readers of the Sunday *Times* drama page. On one occasion I made the unpardonable error of microscopically lettering in the name of Nina's best girl friend, Lisa, the daughter of the distinguished writer, Louis Kronenberger. Well! all hell broke loose on that one. I received telegrams and flowers from forgotten acquaintances and complete strangers: one all the way from Alaska, congratulating my wife and me on the new arrival.

Since then I have confined my nonsense to the single name NINA. I have tried leaving Nina's name out on a couple of occasions but the results were disastrous. Letters poured in with complaints such as: "Where the hell is it?" "My wife says Nina's name is in Ethel Barrymore's hair. We have a bet on it. I say it isn't." "Spent the whole of last Sunday looking for Nina's name but no can find." Etc., etc.

I have learned, the hard way, to put Nina's name in the drawing before I proudly display my own signature simply because the only one who would notice that I had neglected to put my free advertisement in the lower right-hand corner would be me.

Johnny Downs and Joan Roberts in ARE YOU WITH IT? 1945

Max Liebman, Michael Rosenberg, Robert Burton, Imogene Coca, Dorothy Bird, Jules Munshin, Betty Garrett and at extreme right the composer and author respectively, Alex North and Jerry Gury. DANNY DITHER was the musical and it was tried out at Camp Tamiment in the Borscht circuit. 1941

William Prince, Dolly Haas, Bettina Cerf, Robert K. Adams, Harry Gresham, Rosalind Gould and Douglas Rowland returning from a performance at the chocolate city of Hershey, Pennsylvania to the summer theatre home at Eaglesmere, Pennsylvania. The show they played was HER CARDBOARD LOVER; I met the guest star Dolly Haas; I thought she was the greatest actress I had ever seen; I married her. 1940.

George Gershwin's PORGY AND BESS. 1942

The Mack Sennett "chase" ballet in HIGH BUTTON SHOES. 1948

Jose Ferrer in THE SILVER WHISTLE. 1949

Sara Allgood, Barry Fitzgerald and Arthur Shields in JUNO AND THE PAYCOCK. 1940

Al Jolson in his last appearance on Broadway with Martha Raye in HOLD ON TO YOUR HATS. 1940

Ed Wynn, "the perfect fool," in
BOYS AND GIRLS TOGETHER. 1940

Juanita Juarez, Leonard Sues, Romeo Vincent, Jerry Lester, Susan Miller and Jack Whiting in BEAT THE BAND. 1942

Ethel Merman and the three sailors (Frank Hyers, Rags Ragland and Pat Harrington) in PANAMA HATTIE. 1940

Hedi Stenuf, Fritz Dietl, The Four Bruises and Freddie Trenkler in IT HAPPENS ON ICE. 1940

William Gaxton and Victor Moore in LOUISIANA PURCHASE. 1940

Benrimo, playwright, rehearses THE YELLOW JACKET in a summer tryout at Marblehead, Mass. The two thespians are Harpo Marx and Alexander Woollcott. 1941.

Eddie Cantor and friend in BANJO EYES. 1941

Freddie Trenkler in STARS ON ICE. 1943

Edmund Gwenn thought Winston Churchill was
mucking up the war in THE WOOKEY. 1941

Ray Bolger in the revue THREE TO MAKE READY. 1946

Avon Long and Katherine Dunham in CARIB SONG. 1945

Richard Hart, Carol Stone and Marjorie Bell in DARK OF THE MOON. 1945

June Havoc in the musical SADIE THOMPSON. 1944

Lou Holtz, Benny Fields, The De Marcos and The Berry Brothers in STAR TIME. 1944

Gene Sheldon, Lou Holtz, Paul Draper, Hazel Scott and Willie Howard in PRIORITIES OF 1942

Moss Hart recruited his cast from the U.S.
Army for WINGED VICTORY. 1943

Imogene Coca, Salici Puppets, Eddie Mayehoff, Rosario and Antonio,
Katherine Dunham and Zero Mostel in CONCERT VARIETIES. 1945

Frank Fay in HARVEY, Laurette Taylor in THE GLASS MENAGERIE, Judy Holliday
in KISS THEM FOR ME and Frederic O'Neal in ANNA LUCASTA. 1945

Arnold Moss in THE FRONT PAGE. 1946

Irene Manning in a dream sequence with Tom Helmore, Patricia Marshall, Bill Johnson, John Archer, Ralph Glover (Plato) Herman Leopoldi (Freud), Paul Best (Voltaire) and Mary Ellen Moylan in THE DAY BEFORE SPRING. 1945

Frank Craven and Billie Burke in
MRS. JANUARY AND MR. EX. 1944

Victor Moore and William Gaxton with The Hartmans, Hildegarde and Jack Cole in KEEP 'EM LAUGHING. 1942

Ray Bolger, the bouncing comedian in WHERE'S CHARLEY? 1949

Danny Daniels, Joan McCracken, Mitzi Green, David Burns, Robert Chisholm and William Skipper in BILLION DOLLAR BABY. 1945

Shirley Booth, Viola Essen, Victor Moore and William Gaxton in HOLLYWOOD PINAFORE. 1945

Clifton Webb, Mildred Natwick, Leonora Corbett and Peggy Wood in BLITHE SPIRIT. 1941

Elizabeth Bergner and Victor Jory's hand in THE TWO MRS. CARROLLS. 1943

Laurette Taylor and Julie Haydon in THE GLASS MENAGERIE. 1945

Percy Waram and Leo G. Carroll, two Brahmins, in THE LATE GEORGE APLEY. 1945

Victor Jory, Dame May Whitty and Eva Le Gallienne in THERESE. 1945

Leo G. Carroll, Faith Brook, Tom Helmore, Freida Inescort, Patricia Kirkland, Walter Hudd, Nigel Stock and Ralph Forbes in YOU NEVER CAN TELL. 1948

Oscar Karlweis, Annabella, J. Edward Bromberg and Louis Calhern in JACOBOWSKY AND THE COLONEL. 1944

Henry Hull, the Jeeter Lester of the record-breaking TOBACCO ROAD. 1943

George Coulouris in THE INSECT COMEDY. 1948

Mary Wickes, Alan Jones, Florence Lessing, Benny Baker, Betty Garrett, Jerry Lester and Nanette Fabray in JACKPOT. 1944

Sono Osato, Mary Martin, Teddy Hart, Kenny Baker, John Boles and Paula Laurence in the Ogden Nash, Kurt Weill, S. J. Perelman musical ONE TOUCH OF VENUS. 1943

The seven who played Clarence Day in LIFE WITH FATHER from 1939 to 1948. L. to R. Stanley Ridges, Harry Bannister,
A. H. Van Buren, Edwin Cooper, Percy Waram, Howard Lindsay (co-author with Russell Crouse) and Louis Calhern.

Dolly Haas, Lillian Gish and John Gielgud in CRIME AND PUNISHMENT. 1947

"The cakewalk" in Harold Arlen's ST. LOUIS WOMAN. 1946

"The Dance of the Beggars" in THE DYBBUK which the Habima Players brought from Israel. 1948

Maurice Evans and Frances Rowe in MAN AND SUPERMAN with the old master G. B. S. at the controls. 1947

Mae West against a hearts-and-flowers background in DIAMOND LIL. 1949

Flora Robson and Michael Redgrave as Mr. and Mrs. Macbeth. The witches are Robinson Stone, Martin Balsam and Harry Hess, in Shakespeare's MACBETH. 1948

These all played mothers on Broadway in 1949. L. to R. Viola Keats in ANNE OF THE THOUSAND DAYS, Dorothy Stickney in LIFE WITH MOTHER, Mildred Dunnock in DEATH OF A SALESMAN, Adrienne Allen in EDWARD, MY SON and Phyllis Povah in LIGHT UP THE SKY.

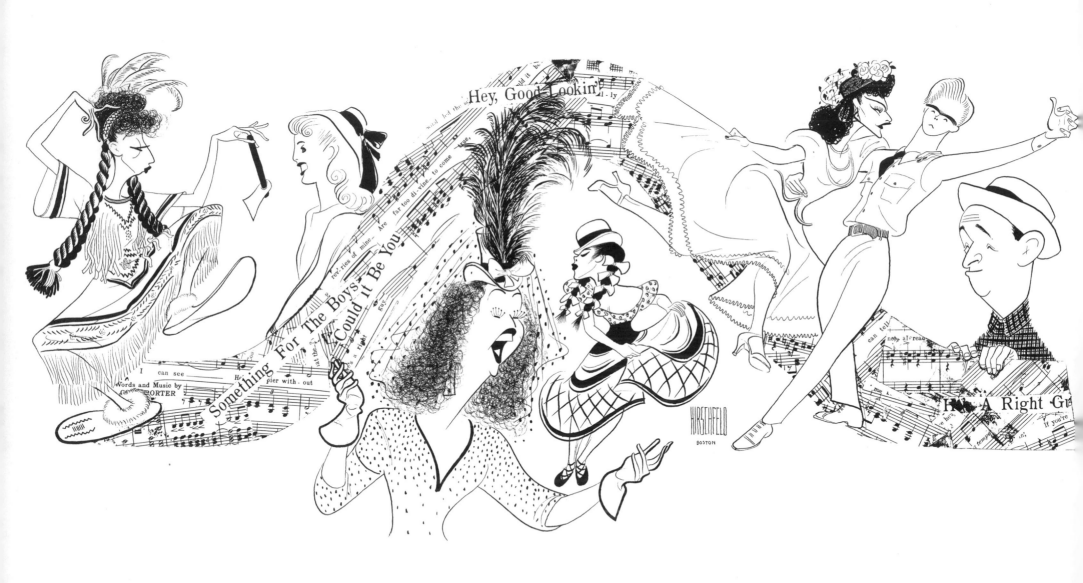

Paula Laurence, Betty Garrett, Ethel Merman, Antia Alvarez, Betty Bruce, Bill Callahan, Allen Jenkins
and a suggestion of some of Cole Porter's singable tunes in SOMETHING FOR THE BOYS. 1943

"The flapper from Little Rock" (Lorelei Lee) empty-headed blonde of the "Twenties" was created in the "Forties" by Carol Channing and her brunette girl friend, Yvonne Adair, in GENTLEMEN PREFER BLONDES. 1949

Burl Ives and Philip Coolidge in SING OUT, SWEET LAND. 1944

Mary Martin and Ezio Pinza rocked the town in SOUTH PACIFIC. 1949

Henry Daniell, Katharine Cornell, Torin Thatcher and Henry Stephenson in THAT LADY. 1949

Hal Sherman, Barto and Mann, "Ole" Olsen and "Chic" Johnson with Shirley Wayne in HELLZAPOPPIN. 1940

Walter Abel, Thomas Mitchell and Russ Brown in THE BIGGEST THIEF IN TOWN. 1949

Una O'Connor and Boris Karloff in THE LINDEN TREE. 1948

Maurice Schwartz, pillar of the Yiddish Art Theatre, in SHYLOCK AND HIS DAUGHTER. 1947

Martita Hunt and Estelle Winwood, two extravagantly sane women, in THE MADWOMAN OF CHAILLOT. 1949

Ethel Waters and Josh White in BLUE HOLIDAY. 1945

Dolly Haas in LUTE SONG. 1946

Bobby Clark, "master of the revels," in AS THE GIRLS GO. 1948

In the Fifties I bought a house in the nineties, and became a staunch defender of the capitalist system. It seemed to me that any economic system so sloppily and benevolently conceived that even I could eventually wind up owning a house could not be all bad.

It all began with a telephone call from S. J. Perelman sometime in the Forties. He suggested we collaborate in the writing of the book for a musical. We met for lunch at the old Lafayette Hotel café that same day. I don't remember what I ate at that luncheon but fifteen years have passed since then and the gas pains are still with me. Our collaboration eventually included lyricist Ogden Nash and composer Vernon Duke.

The four of us labored a couple of years on this foolproof, tightly-knit extravaganza and whelped (from the public point of view) a piece of idiocy titled SWEET BYE AND BYE. The week before this four-hundred-thousand-dollar mish-mash folded in Philadelphia, Perelman and I had lunch with Ted Patrick, the editor of *Holiday Magazine,* at the Warwick Hotel. Patrick, an old friend of Perelman's, made the happy mistake of asking him what his plans were after the contemplated opening in New York. Perelman lackadaisically responded that he was going swordfishing off the Florida coast. Had Patrick called for the check at that moment, I would probably still be living in my reconverted storage space on the roof of an apartment building on West Fifty-Seventh Street.

But Patrick insisted on compounding his original gambit of probing Perelman's plans for the future. He asked if Perelman would care to write a piece for *Holiday* about his adventures in swordfishing. Perelman countered with the suggestion that perhaps Hirschfeld could be included in the deal to illustrate the article. Patrick, a bit more cautious, allowed that maybe it could be worked out, he would give it some thought. I interrupted to announce that, tempting as these proposed plans were, they did not fit into my firm promise to meet my wife and year-and-a-half-old daughter in Hollywood. Dolly, my wife, had been touring on the road in the starring role of LUTE SONG for the past nine months and nothing could sway me from reacquainting myself with my family.

Patrick, throwing reason to the wind, boldly made the proposition that perhaps Perelman could change his plans about swordfishing in Florida, that both of us be despatched to Hollywood to write and draw something about these colorful natives for *Holiday Magazine.* Thus it was that after some additional martinis and insane logical conversation, we were commissioned by Mr. Patrick to *go around the world.* Before the week was out we managed to suck in Simon and Schuster for a fat fee in advance of royalties on a book which turned out to be the best-seller *Westward Ha.*

The accumulated loot from *Holiday* and *Westward Ha* enabled me to buy my house in the nineties in the early Fifties.

Cissy Trenholm, Skippy Baxter, Eileen Seigh and "The Bruises" in an ice show, the title of which made my feet bleed. HOWDY MR. ICE OF 1950.

Jean Arthur and Boris Karloff in PETER PAN. 1950

Mary Martin and Cyril Ritchard in the musical version of PETER PAN. 1954

Henry Lascoe, extreme left, Florence Eldridge waves to Fredric March, standing in coffin, Stephan Schnabel with revolver in NOW I LAY ME DOWN TO SLEEP. 1950

Stuart Erwin, Bambi Linn, Valerie Bettis, J. C. McCord and Vivienne Segal in GREAT TO BE ALIVE. 1950

Uta Hagen (Blanche Du Bois) and Anthony Quinn (Stanley Kowalski) in A STREETCAR NAMED DESIRE. 1950

Maureen Stapleton became part of Tennessee Williams' world in THE ROSE TATTOO. 1951

John Conte, Nanette Fabray, Pearl Bailey and Georges Guetary in ARMS AND THE GIRL. 1950

Michael Wager, Joyce Lear, Dorothy Stickney and Paul McGrath in THE SMALL HOURS. 1951

Two Shaw plays ran concurrently on Broadway, CAESAR AND CLEOPATRA and THE DEVIL'S DISCIPLE. This imaginary cocktail party with teetotaler G. B. S. playing host appeared in 1950. The guests (l. to r.) Bertha Belmore (Ftatateeta), Victor Jory (Anthony Anderson), Lilli Palmer (Cleopatra), John Buckmaster (Apollodorus), Maurice Evans (Dick Dudgeon), G. B. S. (himself), Nicholas Joy (Pothinus), Arthur Treacher (Britannus), Ivan Simpson (Theodotus), Marsha Hunt (Judith), Cedric Hardwicke (Caesar), Ralph Forbes (Rufio), and Dennis King (General Burgoyne).

Julie Harris and Ethel Waters in MEMBER OF THE WEDDING. 1950

Margaret Phillips and Basil Rathbone in Augustus and Ruth Goetz's THE HEIRESS, adapted from Henry James's *Washington Square*. 1950

Gertrude Lawrence and Yul Brynner danced the polka. Yuriko, on opposite page, portrays Eliza's flight from King Simon of Legree in a ballet entitled "The Small House of Uncle Thomas." Hammerstein and Rodgers' THE KING AND I. 1951

Robert Strauss, Donald Foster, Jose Ferrer, Gloria Swanson and William Lynn in TWENTIETH CENTURY. 1951

Douglas Deane, Tom Pedi, Stubby Kaye, John Silver, Robert Alda, Same Levene, B. S. Pully, Vivian Blaine, Pat Rooney, Sr. and Isabel Bigley in GUYS AND DOLLS. 1950

Julie Harris and William Prince in I AM A CAMERA. 1951

Cyril Ritchard, Katharine Hepburn and Robert Helpmann in THE MILLIONAIRESS. 1952

William Marshall as "De Lawd" with his Angels at a celestial fish fry came back to Broadway in Marc Connelly's classic THE GREEN PASTURES. 1951

Roger Furse, the British designer, brought his sets over from England for these two productions of ANTONY AND CLEOPATRA and CAESAR AND CLEOPATRA. Sir Laurence Olivier played Antony and Caesar on alternate nights to Vivien Leigh's Cleopatras. 1951

Phil Silvers and "Sport" Morgan, the singing dog, in TOP BANANA. 1952

Betty Hutton at the Palace. 1952

The Greek National Theatre made its first appearance in the United States with ELECTRA starring Katina Paxinou and her husband Alexis Minotis. 1952

Michael Wager, Mildred Natwick, Anthony Quayle, Torin Thatcher and Katharine Cornell in Christopher Fry's THE FIRSTBORN, brilliantly designed by Boris Aronson. 1958

Paul Lynde, Ronny Graham, Alice Ghostley, Robert Clary, Eartha Kitt, June Carroll and Virginia DeLuce were NEW FACES OF 1952.

Reginald Gardner and Beatrice Lillie in AN EVENING WITH BEATRICE LILLIE. 1952

Nigel Green, Estelle Winwood, Clive Revill, George Howe, Nydia Westman and Sarah Marshall in MR. PICKWICK. 1952

Irwin Corey, Brandon DeWilde, Fred Gwynne, Lydia Reed, Helen Hayes and Jules Munshin in MRS. MC THING. 1952

Jack Cassidy, Sheila Bond (on handle bars) and Paul Valentine in WISH YOU WERE HERE. 1952

Philip Coolidge, Alfred Drake and Beatrice Kraft in KISMET. 1953

Jerry Lewis at the Palace. 1957

Lillian Gish in THE TRIP TO BOUNTIFUL. 1953

Josephine Hull in THE SOLID GOLD CADILLAC. 1953

Nancy Walker in COPPER AND BRASS. 1957

Bobby Van and Vera Zorina recreated the "Slaughter on Tenth Avenue" ballet in the revival of ON YOUR TOES. 1954

Lilo and Gwen Verdon in CAN-CAN. 1953

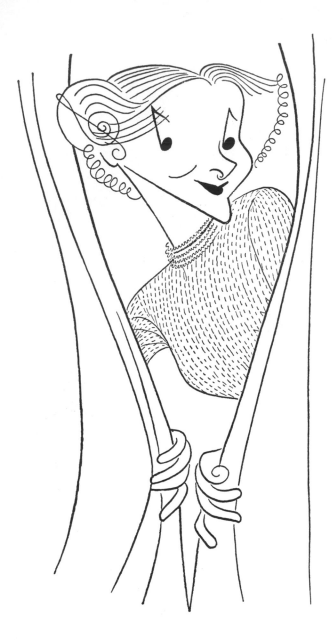

Helen Hayes presented the "Tony" awards at the Plaza Hotel. 1956

J. Carrol Naish, Eileen Heckart, Jack Warden, Gloria Marlowe, Richard Davalos and Van Heflin in Arthur Miller's A VIEW FROM THE BRIDGE. 1955

Lynn Fontanne and Alfred Lunt did a mind-reading act in THE GREAT SEBASTIANS. 1956

Earle Hyman (center) and Josephine Premice (facing him) in MISTER JOHNSON. 1956

L. to R. Hurd Hatfield, Joseph Anthony, Eli Wallach (with boxing gloves), Jenny Goldstein, Jo Van Fleet and Frank Silvera at lower right. Tennessee Williams' CAMINO REAL. 1953

Libby Holman in BLUES, BALLADS AND SIN-SONGS. 1954

Ethel Waters, who makes me cry when she says hello, appeared in a solo performance. 1953

Bradford Dilman, Jason Robards Jr., Florence Eldridge and Fredric March in LONG DAY'S JOURNEY INTO NIGHT. 1956

Gig Young, Franchot Tone and Betsy Von Furstenberg in Edward Chodorov's hilarious comedy OH! MEN, OH! WOMEN. 1954

Paul Muni in INHERIT THE WIND. 1955   Mae Barnes, Robert Jennings, Shirley Booth and Wilbur Evans in BY THE BEAUTIFUL SEA. 1954

Jeanmaire, Brenda Lewis in THE GIRL IN PINK TIGHTS. 1954

Buddy Hackett in LUNATICS AND LOVERS. 1955

Robert Flemyng and Jennifer Jones
in PORTRAIT OF A LADY. 1954

Geraldine Page in THE IMMORALIST. 1954

Jack Palance in THE TEMPEST. 1955

Pat Hingle in THE DARK AT THE TOP
OF THE STAIRS. 1957

A trio of murderers. Patty McCormack, a nine-year-old hoodlum talked it over with her next victim, Henry Jones, in THE BAD SEED. Patricia Jessel and barrister, Francis L. Sullivan in WITNESS FOR THE PROSECUTION. Karl Malden pleads with his son, Malcolm Brodrick while trigger-happy Paul Newman threatens to ventilate the boy's scalp in THE DESPERATE HOURS. 1955

Tyrone Power, Judith Anderson and Raymond Massey in JOHN BROWN'S BODY. 1953

Menasha Skulnik in UNCLE WILLY. 1956

David Opatoshu, Henry Lascoe, Leon Belasco, Hildegarde Neff, Don Ameche and Philip Sterling in SILK STOCKINGS. 1955

Mariko Niki, David Wayne and John Forsythe in TEAHOUSE OF THE AUGUST MOON. 1959

John Wyse, Lynn Fontanne and Alfred Lunt in THE VISIT. 1958

Ken LeRoy and Mickey Calin, switch-blade street fighters, stage a "rumble" for the first-act finale of WEST SIDE STORY. The star-crossed lovers, stage center, are Larry Kert and Carol Lawrence. 1957

Boy meets girl in Hong Kong "house of joy." The girl France Nuyen, the boy William Shattner—the play, THE WORLD OF SUZIE WONG. 1958

East meets East in THE FLOWER DRUM SONG. Pat Suzuki does a strip-tease in a San Francisco fleabag while Miyoshi Umeki, newly arrived mail-order bride from China, looks on. 1958

Jo Sullivan, Scott Merrill, Lotte Lenya, Jane Connell, Tige Andrews and a quartet of professional beggars in Kurt Weill's THE THREEPENNY OPERA. 1955 and still going strong.

Zero Mostel as Leopold Bloom and other characters brought to life from James Joyce's *Ulysses* in ULYSSES IN NIGHTTOWN. 1958

Asia Mercoolova "bumps" her way across stage in WHOOP UP. This drawing appears here for the first time due to a newspaper strike in December of 1958.

Myron McCormick, Gloria Vanderbilt, Harold Lang and Franchot Tone in William Saroyan's THE TIME OF YOUR LIFE. 1955

Judy Holliday and Sydney Chaplin in BELLS ARE RINGING. 1956

Rosalind Russell in AUNTIE MAME. 1956

Robert Helpmann and Moira Shearer in A MIDSUMMER NIGHT'S DREAM. 1954

Anthony Quayle arrived from Toronto, Canada, with his production of TAMBURLAINE THE GREAT. 1956

Judy Garland at the Palace sings "Get Happy." 1956

Marcel Marceau becomes a butterfly and, at right, fights his way through an imagined wind storm. 1956

Harry Belafonte, Marge and Gower Champion in THREE FOR TONIGHT. 1955

The summer theatres in 1956 saw these sophisticated ladies in their own productions touring the citronella circuit. Mae West, Tallulah Bankhead, Beatrice Lillie and Hermione Gingold.

Eric Portman and Margaret Leighton in SEPARATE TABLES. Left, as they appeared in the first act of the twin bill; center, drawn in their dressing rooms during intermission; right, as they appeared transformed for the second act. 1957

Julie Harris in THE COUNTRY WIFE. 1957

Shelley Berman, Bert Lahr and Nancy Walker in THE GIRLS AGAINST THE BOYS. 1959

Alec McCowan, Eileen Herlie, Rosamund Greenwood, Arthur Hill, Ruth Gordon,
Peter Bayliss, Loring Smith and Patrick McAlinney in THE MATCHMAKER. 1955

Judy Garland at the Metropolitan Opera. 1959

Tony Randall played a split personality in OH CAPTAIN! 1958

Edward G. Robinson in THE MIDDLE OF THE NIGHT. 1956

Mildred Natwick and Ralph Richardson in THE WALTZ OF THE TOREADORS. 1957

Arnold Moss portrayed G.B.S. and Valerie Bettis, the
eternal serpent in BACK TO METHUSELAH. 1958

Wendy Hiller and Franchot Tone in A MOON FOR THE MISBEGOTTEN. 1957

Christopher Plummer, Raymond Massey and Pat Hingle in J.B. Designed by Boris Aronson. 1958

Anne Bancroft and Henry Fonda in TWO FOR THE SEESAW. 1958

Maureen Stapleton, Cliff Robertson and Lois Smith in ORPHEUS DESCENDING. 1957

Horst Bucholz and Kim Stanley with Edith King, Lucy Landau and Lili Darvas in Anita Loos' adaptation of two Colette novels titled CHERIE. 1959

Paul Newman and Geraldine Page equipped with marijuana, whiskey, a "family" sized oxygen tank, respirator, and a tape recorder (partly visible) shack up in a Southern hotel for a "cool" love scene in SWEET BIRD OF YOUTH. 1959

Orson Welles in the title role of KING LEAR. 1956

Ethel Merman in HAPPY HUNTING. 1956

Good relations between the Bronx and Tokyo were established with Gertrude Berg and Sir Cedric Harwicke in A MAJORITY OF ONE. 1959

Kurt Kasznar, Alvin Epstein, Bert Lahr and E. G. Marshall in Samuel Beckett's tragicomedy WAITING FOR GODOT. 1956

Heller Halliday, Don Murray, Mary Martin, Helen Hayes, George Abbott and Florence Reed pooled their talents to produce Thornton Wilder's THE SKIN OF OUR TEETH for the Theatre Festival in Paris. 1955

Herbert Berghof, Albert Dekker, Ian Keith and George C. Scott in THE ANDERSONVILLE TRIAL. 1959

Marcel Pagnol's *Cesar* trilogy was adapted by Harold Rome into FANNY. L. to R. William Tabbert, Walter Slezak, Florence Henderson and Ezio Pinza. 1954

Jeremy Brett, Rosemary Harris, Ronald Allen, Coral Browne, Paul Rogers and John Neville in Tyrone Guthrie's Edwardian conception of TROILUS AND CRESSIDA produced by the Old Vic Company from London. 1956

Cameron Prud'homme, Gwen Verdon, Thelma Ritter and George Wallace did a musical version of O'Neill's *Anna Christie* titled NEW GIRL IN TOWN. 1957

Eric Portman, Betty Field, Helen Hayes and Kim Stanley in the sensibly named Helen Hayes Theatre with O'Neill's A TOUCH OF THE POET. 1958

A musical adaptation of Jane Austen's *Pride and Prejudice* became FIRST IMPRESSIONS with Hermione Gingold, Farley Granger, Polly Bergen and James Mitchell. 1959

Joseph Cotten and Margaret Sullavan in SABRINA FAIR. 1959

Josephine Premice, Lena Horne and Ricardo Montalban in JAMAICA. 1957

Ray Walston, Stephen Douglass, Gwen Verdon and some Bob Fosse ball players in DAMN YANKEES. 1955

Roddy McDowall, George Baker, Tammy Grimes and Kurt Kasznar in Noel Coward's LOOK AFTER LULU. 1959

Lauren Bacall and Sydney Chaplin in GOODBYE CHARLIE. 1959

Jose Ferrer in CYRANO. 1953

This drawing was used as a front curtain in the English importation AT THE DROP OF A HAT. The total cast comprised two men, one, a bearded gentleman in a wheel chair and the other, a madman at the piano. Their names? Flanders and Swann. 1959

An off-Broadway theatre audience relaxes during intermission. 1956

Bette Davis in TWO'S COMPANY. 1952

Ruth Ford, Zachary Scott and Beatrice Reading in REQUIEM FOR A NUN. 1959

Jerome Cowan, Johnny Desmond, Horace McMahon, Robert Morse, David Wayne and Vivian Blaine in SAY, DARLING. 1958

Rex Harrison in THE FIGHTING COCK. 1959   Eartha Kitt in MRS. PATTERSON. 1954

Gloria Vanderbilt in THE SWAN. 1954

Howard Lindsay and Dorothy Stickney as Clarence and Vinnie Day in a revival of LIFE WITH FATHER. 1954

Marc Breaux, George Reeder, Swen Swenson, Dolores Gray and Andy Griffith in DESTRY RIDES AGAIN. 1959

Jack Klugman, Ethel Merman, Sandra Church and a trio of inventive strip-teasers in GYPSY. 1959

Robert Preston, and at right, David Burns, Helen Raymond, Pert Kelton and Barbara Cook in THE MUSIC MAN. 1957

Matt Mattox and Carol Channing in THE VAMP. 1955

Julie Andrews and some John Held, Jr. creations brought to life in the English importation THE BOY FRIEND. 1955

Cozy Cole and Muriel Smith in Billy Rose's colorful CARMEN JONES. 1956

Sir Laurence Olivier graced our stage in THE ENTERTAINER. 1958

The foolhardy task of adapting G. B. Shaw's *Pygmalion* into a musical was attempted by Lerner and Loewe. Moss Hart tried to stage it. Three British actors were engaged (depicted above) Stanley Holloway, Julie Andrews and Rex Harrison. It turned into the "American" classic MY FAIR LADY. 1956

Gwen Verdon cavorted in varied guises in the murder-mystery musical REDHEAD. 1959

Pierre Olaf (France's gift to the American Theatre), with three companions flew through the air in "The Bell Ringing Scene," a comic masterpiece, in LA PLUME DE MA TANTE. 1959

Danny Kaye at the Palace. 1953

THE ?IXTIE?

The notable theatrical events so far, in this new decade, have taken place mostly outside of the professional theatre. Robert Frost read his poem at President Kennedy's inaugural in Washington and the rostrum caught fire. FBI security agents rushed to the rescue and in full view of the TV audience (probably the largest ever assembled in the world's history) put out the fire by pouring ginger ale on it.

I speculated at the time on the various ways this spectacle would have been staged in other countries. In England, they probably would have removed Mr. Frost to a place of safety and then carted off the burning rostrum. In the Soviet Union, they no doubt would have arrested Mr. Frost. In France, the Pompiers would have perhaps just peed on the fire.

Other highlights of the past seasons have been Castro's performance up at the Hotel Thérèse in Harlem and Premier Khrushchev's balcony scene from the second-floor porch of the Soviet Embassy on Park Avenue. Both of these turns have been (to borrow an adjective from Brooks Atkinson) "rewarding." But undoubtedly the most dramatic off-Broadway extravaganza so far has been the staggering production of shooting a man into outer space.

In the ensuing years I expect to find myself, on alternate weeks, either in New Haven, Boston, Philadelphia or Washington, making sketches of a show to be correlated into a design for the Sunday drama section of *The New York Times*. If my ink bottle holds out and the patience of my editors endures I intend to continue this procedure until space sends a man for me.

HENRY V in Central Park. James Ray played the title role in New York's Shakespeare Festival. 1960

Anne Revere, Jason Robards Jr., Maureen Stapleton and Irene Worth in Lillian Hellman's TOYS IN THE ATTIC. 1960

Tom Ewell and Paul Ford on a drunken Christmas-shopping spree in THE THURBER CARNIVAL. 1960

Maurice Evans and Ron Husmann, at extreme right, register shock and amusement at the goings on in a local whorehouse, circa 1890, in Manhattan's colorful West Side aptly titled TENDERLOIN. 1960

Dick Van Dyke, Chita Rivera, Susan Watson (teen-age telephone addict), Dick Gautier (rock 'n' roll idol),
Kay Medford and Paul Lynde (Mom and Dad) in Gower Champion's expertly directed BYE BYE BIRDIE. 1960

Kenneth Haigh (top), directly below is Colleen Dewhurst and sporting a luxuriant beard is Philip Bourneuf in Sidney Lumet's sumptuous spectacle CALIGULA. 1960

And from Japan came GRAND KABUKI with Kanzaburo, Utaemon and Shoroku. 1960

A quartet of European plays appeared simultaneously on Broadway. Celia Salkeld, Alfred Lynch and Glynn Edwards in THE HOSTAGE. Angela Lansbury and Joan Plowright in A TASTE OF HONEY. Elizabeth Seal in IRMA LA DOUCE. Anthony Quinn and Laurence Olivier in BECKET. 1960

The villains of current shows in 1960. Herbert Berghof in THE ANDERSONVILLE TRIAL, Stephan Gierasch in THE SOUND OF MUSIC, Marc Breaux, George Reeder, Swen Swenson and Art Lund in DESTRY RIDES AGAIN, Leonard Stone in REDHEAD, and Jane White in ONCE UPON A MATTRESS.

Tammy Grimes, Harve Presnell, Edith Meiser, Mony Dalmes and Mitchell Gregg in THE UNSINKABLE MOLLY BROWN. 1960

Bruce MacKay, Ellen McCown, William Chapman, John Megna, Cecil Kellaway, Anthony Perkins, Lee Cass and Pert Kelton in the bucolic musical GREENWILLOW. 1960

Laurence Olivier and Anthony Quinn in BECKET. 1960

Richard Burton, Julie
Andrews, Robert Goulet
and Roddy McDowall in
CAMELOT. 1960

Keith Andes, Lucille Ball and Don Tomkins in WILDCAT. 1960

George Mathews, George Givot and David Burns (table at left). John Reardon and Nancy Dussault (center table). Phil Silvers and Nancy Walker at extreme right. In DO RE MI. Boris Aronson did a masterful job in designing this production. 1960

Carol Channing brought back the
Twenties in SHOW GIRL. 1961

The inimitable Elsa Lanchester. 1961

Hurd Hatfield, Michael Mac Liammoir, John Gielgud, Margaret Leighton, Donald Moffat and George Rose in MUCH ADO ABOUT NOTHING. 1960

Eric Christmas, Sig Ruman, Walter Matthau, Françoise Rosay, Carol Grace and Julie Newmar in ONCE THERE WAS A RUSSIAN. 1961

Frank Lovejoy, Melvyn Douglas and Lee Tracy in THE BEST MAN. 1960

Martin Gabel (sybarite), Hume Cronyn (pansy) and Jason Robards Jr. (an AC-DC fellow) in BIG FISH, LITTLE FISH. 1961

Ludwig Donath, Carol Lawrence and Theodore Bikel in THE DYBBUK. Play of the Week. 1960

The Phoenix Players in HENRY IV at the Phoenix Theatre. 1960

Myron McCormick and Jason Robards Jr. in O'Neill's
THE ICEMAN COMETH. Play of the Week. 1960

Carol Lawrence, Oscar Homolka and Ricardo Montalban in RASHOMON. Play of the Week. 1960

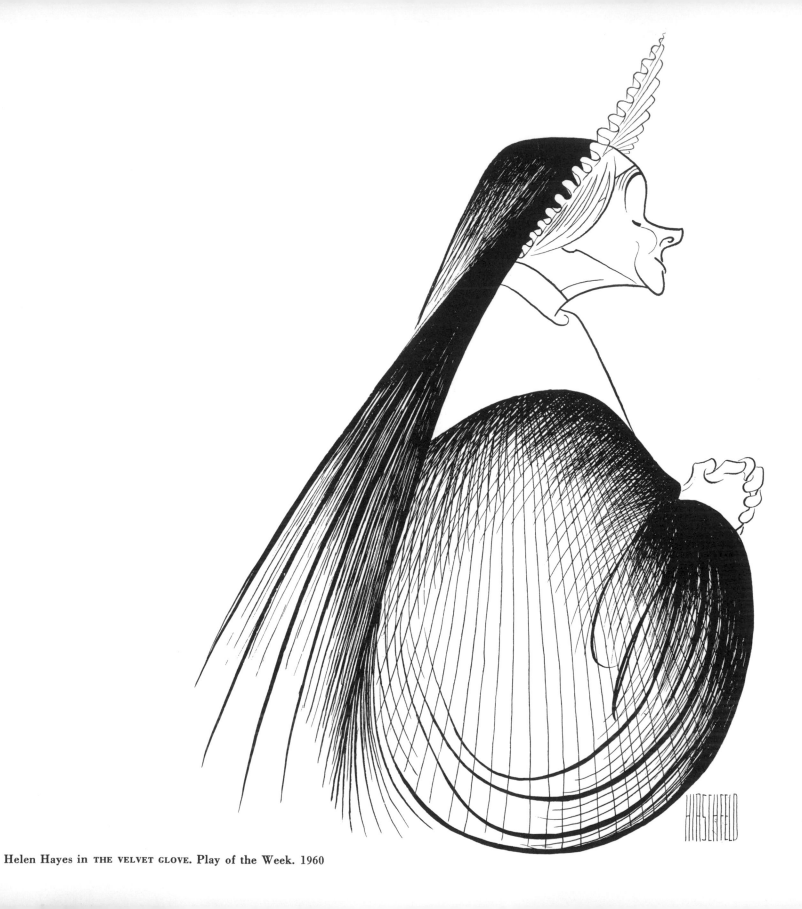

Helen Hayes in THE VELVET GLOVE. Play of the Week. 1960

Burgess Meredith and Zero Mostel in WAITING FOR GODOT. Play of the Week. 1960

Tallulah Bankhead flew through the air with the greatest of ease in MIDGIE PURVIS. 1961

Janice Rule on an Olympian cloud. Cyril Ritchard descends to his Satanic underworld. The lovers are Dran Seitz and Bruce Yarnell in THE HAPPIEST GIRL IN THE WORLD. 1961

Sylvia Syms, Monica Boyar, Don Ameche, Richard Tone and Isabelle Farrell in the first musical from our new state of Hawaii, THIRTEEN DAUGHTERS. 1961

Pierre Olaf, Jerry Ohrbach, Anna Maria Alberghetti, Kaye Ballard and James Mitchell in CARNIVAL. Staged by Gower Champion. 1961

Zero Mostel, using no theatrical devices other than an actor's mind, becomes a rhinoceros and attacks Eli Wallach in Ionesco's satire, RHINOCEROS. 1961

. . . and one more from The Forties on the next page.

This drawing placed at the end of this book is also a visual record of the end of my career as a playwright.

THE SCENE: The Hotel Warwick, Philadelphia.

CAST OF CHARACTERS: S. J. Perelman, Al Hirschfeld, Vernon Duke and Ogden Nash.

THE PLAY: SWEET BYE AND BYE*

*see chapter THE FORTIES.

Earl Wilson, N. Y. Post   Mr. & Mrs. Leonard Lyons, N. Y. Post   Mr. & Mrs. Martin Gable
                                                                                (Arlene Francis)   Howard Cullman
          Robert Sylvester, N. Y. Daily News   Mr. & Mrs. Moss Hart   Robert Dowling
Ed Sullivan, N. Y. Daily News   Louis Sobol, N. Y. Journal-American   (Kitty Carlisle)   Mr. & Mrs. Sidney Lumet
                                                                         (Gloria Vanderbilt)   Roger Stevens
          George S. Kaufman   Truman Capote   Robert Whitehead   Mr. & Mrs. William Zeckendorf